"that
pestilent
cosmetic,
rhetoric"

"that pestilent cosmetic, rhetoric"

by
SOL CHANELES
&
JEROME SNYDER

GROSSMAN PUBLISHERS / NEW YORK / 1972

COPY 3

EUCHARISTA

GRATIARUM ACTIO to all authors, publishers, and magazines for permission
to use the following excerpts from copyrighted material:

Commentary: From Paul Goodman's article that appeared in the July 1971
issue. Copyright © 1971 by The American Jewish Committee. Reprinted by
permission.

Doubleday & Co. Inc.: From *Story of My Life* by Helen Keller

Harper & Row, Publishers, Inc.: From *The Passionate State of Mind*
by Eric Hoffer. (Harper & Row, Publishers, Inc. 1954) and from
Excellence by John W. Gardner. (Harper & Row, Publishers, Inc. 1964)

New Directions Publishing Corporation and J. M. Dent & Sons Ltd.:
From *Quite Early One Morning* by Dylan Thomas. Copyright 1954 by
New Directions Publishing Corporation. New Directions Publishing
Corporation and International Famous Agency for "The Timeless World
of a Play," introduction to *The Rose Tattoo*, by Tennessee Williams.
Copyright 1950, 1951 by Tennessee Williams. Reprinted by permission.

Playboy: From *Playboy Philosophy.* Reproduced by special permission
of *Playboy* Magazine; Copyright © 1962, 1963, 1964, 1965 by Playboy.

Random House, Inc.: From William Faulkner's Nobel Prize Acceptance
Speech, from *The Faulkner Reader.* Copyright 1950 by William Faulkner.

Saturday Review: From an excerpt from an article by John Ciardi

Anagkeon & Deisis
Any errors or omissions that may have inadvertently occurred will
be corrected in subsequent editions of this book upon notification
to the authors.

This book was set on linotype in Bodoni
by H. Wolff Book Manufacturing Co., New York.
The printing and binding is by Halliday Lithograph Corp.
Designed by Gertrude Snyder.

a view of the rhetor

"He is skillful in Rhetorick, which gives a speech colour, as Logick doth favour, and both together beauty. Though some condemne Rhetorick as the mother of lies, speaking more than the truth in Hyperboles, lesse in her miosis, otherwise in her metaphors, contrary in her ironies; yet is there excellent use of all these, when disposed of with judgement."

THOMAS FULLER, *The Holy State*, Book II, Chapter 7

Every dissolute intriguer, loose-liver, forger, false-coiner, and prison-bird; every hare-brained, loud-talking dema- gogue; every speculator, scoffer and atheist, — was a fol- lower of Jefferson; and Jefferson was himself the incarnation of their theories.

Harsh? Impolitic? Hardly! One hundred years after Henry Adams, great-grandson of the second Presi- dent of the United States, delivered himself of this broad- side against the third, beleaguered New York City's youthful mayor, John Vliet Lindsay, heard the Irish brogue of transit boss Michael J. Quill taunt him thus:

You are nothing but a juvenile, a lightweight and a pipsqueak. You have to grow up.

Both remarks are widely regarded as eminently fair — honored by at least two thousand years of tradition.

Words are man's most powerful tools for persua- sion. They comprise the chief medium through which people influence other people's behavior.

Words are more economical than either violence or bribery. Except on paper, no village has ever been razed, no dreams laid waste, or bodies incinerated by polysyllables. Four-letter words sting but do not destroy.

At the very least, rhetoric is all the reasons for using words: it is the bag of crafty tricks for common word-mongers; it is the sublime esthetic for the consum- mate orator; it is the repertoire of homilies for pietists and the source of the sage commonplaces of elder statesmen. Words are acts of aggrandizement — rhetoric their tac- tical plan — to bring out into strong relief some aspect of truth which would not be clear otherwise. Whatsoever is certain needs no persuasion, it is closed to rhetoric.

To inveigh against their opponents, Henry Adams and Michael Quill used a squelch or *bdelygmia* as the ancient Greeks called this rhetorical figure. Aristotle's fellow Athenians and public speakers long before them were well versed in verbal devices for putting people down. Politicians, generally, employ more Squelches than Uplifts. Uplifting speech is usually reserved for ribbon-cutting ceremonies, fund-raising dinners, funerals, and other settings for panegyric.

> *Men are much less willing to have their weaknesses and their imperfections known than their crimes; and if you hint to a man that you think him silly, ignorant, or even ill-bred or awkward, he will hate you more and longer than if you tell him plainly that you think him a rogue.* **LORD CHESTERFIELD**

Beginning in the 1960's it became fashionable to bdelygmize* the term "rhetoric" itself. Public speakers, lacking a substantive basis for criticizing their opponents, found it convenient to accuse them of "rhetoric." This trick calls to mind Monsieur Jourdain, Molière's *Bourgeois Gentilhomme,* who discovered to his considerable surprise and delight that he had been speaking prose all his life. He could equally have decided that he was speaking rhetoric, for all speech, all communication that has a purpose is, indeed, rhetoric. To imply that public utterance is rhetoric and therefore something derogatory is to defame thought and its expression. It is a low trick of the demagogue. Cicero, Quintilian, and Saint Augustine — students, practitioners, and codifiers of rhetoric — would have unleashed a flood of *mycterismos* at the abusers of rhetoric's good name. They, among others, raised the principles and practices of rhetoric to the level of science and high art. People who recognize rhetoric as "hot" or "cool" deserve tribute for their perceptiveness, for the scale of temperature evoked by words is precisely what rhetoric is about.

---

* When no proper term is available, it is a perfectly legitimate practice to coin a word; the rhetorical term for such a practice is *catachresis.*

The more informed the reader or listener, the greater the demand upon the rhetor's ingenuity. Rhetors must know what provokes anger, admiration, shame, pride, determination, compassion. They must be able to make distinctions among settings for discourse and distinguish among audiences: the young, old, humble and well-born, the fiercely partisan and the apathetic. Rhetors of old went about, often alone, speaking their mind to gatherings on country roads, in marketplaces, in public squares, and in architecturally elaborate forums. The contemporary rhetor is seldom alone: he is a veritable manufacturer of rhetoric, employer of scores of advance men, publicists, speech writers, make-up specialists, television technicians, prompters, claques, and voice coaches. And to determine what should be said to whom, where, and on what occasion, public-opinion pollsters have become a major stage-setting force for public utterance. All this — indispensable! For words, like people, are ever in flux.

> *A word is not a crystal, transparent and unchanged, it is the skin of a living thought and may vary greatly in color and content according to the circumstances and time in which it is used.* JUSTICE OLIVER WENDELL HOLMES

We should rejoice whenever we are targets of rhetoric. It matters little who covets our minds on behalf of causes, products, and amusements, even little wars; whoever does so flatters us and needs us. Without our support, verbal coveters must inevitably fail in their persuasive purpose.

Rhetoric is the logic, the time-honored plan, for stating purposes and convincing people of their merit. Without rhetoric there is silence — and tyranny.

Rhetoric may be sinister but expressed with such sweetness and sincerity (*paradiastole*) that what is said is merely a disguise for devious intentions. Obviously, we are pleased when people, especially public figures, state their purposes openly. When they do not, we owe it to ourselves to set aside their words, measuring only their actions. But this is risky, for the hangman lulls us with soft words as he slips the noose around our necks. Prudence demands that we beware the man who acts on our behalf without a clear prior statement of his intention: the deed should match the word. A man who acts without declaration is either trying to pull the wool over our eyes or is profoundly ignorant of what he is doing.

Secrecy in a democracy is abhorrent. Thus, among the Athenians, rhetoric was the principal subject matter taught to future leaders. Its mastery was the hallmark of civility and morality. Many different schools of rhetoric flourished in Athens, contending and competing for dominance. Some were wedded to the conviction that the epitome of rhetorical excellence depended on condensation, brevity of expression — a truth in the fewest possible words. Other schools promoted extensive elaboration and variety. There were advocates of bare-knuckle directness as well as devotees of florid circumlocution — but all shared a single objective: persuasion through reasoned words as opposed to coercion through chains. Of all the features of Athenian democracy the conquering Romans might have borrowed, they adopted rhetoric first, then applied it rigorously.

Public rhetoric cannot convey all that is on the speaker's mind. Full disclosure of purpose and meaning is possible only in the scientist's laboratory and the lover's nest. Failure of full disclosure in the laboratory might lead to the blowing up of a scientist or, for the lover, the blowing of a mind. The public speaker implies reservations and qualifications, suggests a plethora of alternatives even when there are but a handful. The rhetor diverts, digresses, and often dissimulates in order to score. Over four hundred techniques have come down through the millennia to assist the speaker in his tasks.

Consider the following purpose of the "New

Frontier" as the late President John F. Kennedy put it:

> *Let it be clear that this administration recognizes the value of dissent and daring, that we greet healthy controversy as the hallmark of healthy change.*

Among the rhetorical figures used in this excerpt from the 1960 Inauguration speech are *prolepsis, parimion,* and *hypozeuxis.* But it is the meaning rather than the form of the hypozeuxis that reveals Kennedy's purpose. *"Greet"* suggests *welcome;* that is, dissent will be looked upon favorably, and recognized. But JFK avoids saying it will be agreed to. A little something for everyone.

Kennedy's purpose, however, is moral and indeed noble: to generate hope for something new, bold, welcoming open-mindedness to the winds of change he hoped to set in motion. Using some of the same rhetorical figures, adding a few of his own, Justice William Douglas takes up the issue of dissent head-on:

> *Violence has no constitutional sanction; and every government from the beginning has moved against it. But where grievances pile high and most of the elected spokesmen represent the Establishment, violence may be the only effective response.*

Kennedy transformed the abrasive issue of dissent into an uplifting *prototrope* — an appeal to the untried promise of his governance. Justice Douglas holds out no hope against violence and delivers a firm *paraenesis* — a grim warning.

Cheers eventually subside, applause dims, tears dry; when the emotional response to rhetoric abates, the audience often forgets what words were spoken. When verbal thrusts are done, it is up to the audience to act upon truth in its own way, by word or action. Sometimes the cues to action are not well-wrought phrases like "Martin, Barton and Fish," "Blood, Sweat and Tears," or "the military-industrial complex," but a flowing bow tie, an inflection, a wave of the hand, a roll of the eyes toward heaven, or a dazzling display of teeth. The audience may remember only the clamor and noise, not the meaning or purpose. One of the greatest modern orators, William Jennings Bryan, who swayed millions of listeners into political action, is no longer remembered for his powerful phrases. He is compared, instead, to the Platte River of his native Nebraska — *"Five inches deep and five miles wide at the mouth."* Another modern orator, whose half-century of devotion to the commonweal has left an uncommon, bountiful legacy to unborn generations, is derided for his rhetorical style:

> *Lesser oratory, venal, hypocritical, in defense of the indefensible, is patently factitious, its free language a cosmetic, a youthful roseate complexion arranged on an old, shrewd and degenerated visage as in . . . the tediously predictable alliterated triads of Everett McKinley Dirkson.* JOHN ILLO

Rhetoric's golden age spanned a thousand years. It began in Sicily in 400 B.C., peaking out in Carthage around A.D. 400. During that period, the great codifiers of Rhetoric — Corax, Aristotle, Cicero, Quintilian, and St. Augustine — developed exhaustive categories of things people believed in so that speakers might choose from among them the ones they stood a good chance to promote successfully. Audience reaction tests used by market researchers and the techniques of opinion pollsters are only present-day applications of ancient concepts and devices. *Aposiopesis* (arousing passion for a thing or person), a prime instrument of persuasion for boob-tube lawyers, was equally popular among the young barristers in the circle of Cicero. Now, as then, this figure, like most rhetorical figures, is valid for the rabble as well as the elite, as valid for promoting policies toward China as it is for promoting chewing gum.

Rhetoric is the "science of speaking well," said Quintilian around 55 B.C., adding that the goal of communication is persuasion. Even simple, unadorned communication requires a measure of persuasive intent to produce enough trust so that one may act as speaker or listener. In the fourth book of *De Doctrina Christiana*, St. Augustine boils the issue down to this assertion:

> *A man is persuaded by speech if . . . he likes what you promise, fears what you say is imminent, hates what you censure, embraces what you command . . . and in whatever other ways your high eloquence can affect the minds of your hearers, bringing them not merely to know what should be done, but to do what they know should be done.*

"The Age of Rhetoric," wrote Thomas De Quincy, supreme master of English rhetoric, over a century ago, *"like that of chivalry has passed amongst forgotten things."* Not so! Most universities no longer teach rhetoric as broadly or intensively as it was taught by Erasmus of Rotterdam in 1500, but this fact indicates little since less and less is taught nowadays in these centers of misinformation. Rhetoric is much with us, often called by a variety of names: advertising, propaganda, rapping, dialogue, confrontation, and, on occasion, speech.

Rhetoric lifts us up, puts us down, tells us how to tease, how to soothe, how to find a verbal counterhold for every hold, to defend against every linguistic attack, to offer disproof for every proof, and for every vituperation, a praise that matches it. Its strength is logic, its beauty, eloquence, its brain, appropriateness. There is no greater rhetorical vice than an utterance that matches neither its audience nor its occasion.

For the brief period of a century, 1500-1600, Rhetoric enjoyed an intense revival of interest. A new wave of compilers, codifiers, and declaimers appeared in the European courts and centers of scholarship. Too many of them, however, were ascetics, timid moralists concerned not with the enlargement of reason with arguments that challenged the official line of authority, but with the mass dissemination of church doctrine calculated to produce acquiescence to authority. The result — voluminous adages, maxims, proverbs, and "thoughts" that have, over time, entered our collective common wisdom and everyday language. And when the marketplace of ideas was flooded with snippets of pithy sayings, still bigger compilations became necessary — making encyclopedias inevitable.

The rise of modern states, conflicting ideologies, rapacious competition for minds, souls, and pocketbooks have brought about a recrudescence of rhetoric. The rigorous demands of electronic communications, mass addiction to daily newspapers and popular magazines, a growing international climate of skepticism toward all forms of traditional authority and especially toward spokesmen for vested interests all have contributed toward the generation of new standards of what is appropriate. Speaker and writer have responded through a quickened interest in the most effective ways to advocate. We have moved into the Age of Advocacy, its prime instrument — rhetoric.

Cicero once said: *"I have thought long and often over the problem whether the power of speaking and the study of eloquence have brought more good or harm to men and cities."* Upon reflection, Cicero decided that eloquence should be combined with wisdom and that good and wise people should not leave political life to the clever and bad, but should acquire a mastery of rhetoric to make themselves effective. The ideal person is one who possesses high virtue and the eloquence to adorn it. He concludes: *"Only a good man can speak well."*

why Greek?

Of the more than four hundred verbal instruments making up the armamentarium of rhetoric, only

13

about a hundred have been included in this guide. The curious or vexatious reader will ask why. Our reply: some major rhetorical devices require illustration of such length or are so unadaptable to everyday discourse that they fall outside the realm of what we consider appropriate for this book. *Drama*, for example, is a rhetorical figure demanding extended exposition by means of conversation. The rhetoric of dramaturgy inexorably struts with us on life's stage, and, in turn, we play games with one another, are fitfully theatrical, play to the galleries with our small agonies, large joys, and hand-wringing on the apron. *Drama* has been excluded, and for the same reason we have not included *Comedia* (a species of *Drama*), the *Epithalamion* (a wedding poem), *Fabella* (see Aesop), *Genethliaca* (a poetic form extolling the birth of notable people), *Oaristys* (poetry in praise of marital bliss), or poems in praise of teachers (*Padeuteria*), heroes (*Palinodia*), or departed friends in a form descriptive of the farewell voyage (*Propempticon*).

Many of the four hundred or more rhetorical devices have not been included because they are worthy neither of emulation nor self-instruction. Some define serious faults of expression, which should be avoided at all costs, like *Bomphiologia* (bombast) or *Cacemphaton* (harsh, disagreeable sounds); others dwell on picayune points of grammatical construction: *Cacosyntheton* (a bad arrangement of words), *Hysterologia* (a misplaced preposition), *Pichiologia* (an otherwise deserving expression faulted by overexuberance).

Finally, regarding exclusion from this guide, we have omitted numerous rhetorical devices that are but minor variations upon major figures of speech. For example, *Audacia* and *Superlatio* are skimpy tools for exaggeration, diminished, indeed demolished, by the elegant, noble *Hyperbole* in whose shadow they pretend. The vigorous *Asyndeton* overpowers her puny, distant cousin *Dialyton*, and the euphonious *Symploche* serves her ends more precisely than the variant *Conduplicatio*.

This is all well and good, you say, but why Greek? Why are the figures, defined and illustrated in this guide, presented in their original Greek nomenclature? There are several reasons. First, the pioneer rhetors were Greek; simple propriety suggests tribute to the founding fathers. We have, second, avoided our own tongue because common English usage is generally devoid of names for rhetorical figures, and the relatively few that are in use — alliteration, irony, acclamation, rejection, suavity, concession, attribution, allusion, urbanity, and so on, good rhetorical figures all — have, over time, developed meanings too narrow or connotations too strong to be useful in this book. It is for the same reason that Latin rhetorical nomenclature was not used: Latin is too close to English to avoid unwarranted meanings or feelings. For example, *Abominatio* is so close to the repugnant suggestion of our own English term "abomination" that we preferred the emotionally neutral and original Greek term for the figure, *Bdelygmia*. For the same reason we preferred to use the term *Aposiopesis*, rather than its Latin equivalent, *Reticentia*, since the latter would improperly call to mind our "reticence," a far cry from the essence of that splendid figure.

We could have used numbers:

┇┇0 2 ┞0┉000 2┇┇ 008┉0┉0┞ ┞9 3 2┇┉

but what they enjoy in precision, they lack in meaning.

We could have used the synthetic languages of the electronic computers, the color gradations used in spectroanalysis, or even botanical, chemical, and biological taxonomies; but while all these are valid languages, specialized languages, they have little or no correspondence to the primordial need of humanity — mutual understanding among all men in all stations of life. No contrived language can cause men to reason, be persuaded, or moved to action.

That's why.

squelch
&
uplift

bdelygmia

bē-del-ig'mi-a

A litany of abuse.

William Hazlitt on the Public:

There is no more mean, stupid, dastardly, pitiful, self-ish, spiteful, envious, ungrateful animal than the public. It is the greatest of cowards, for it is afraid of itself.

Spiro Agnew on the Press:

[Law abiding Americans] . . . need a strong voice to penetrate the cacaphony of seditious drivel emanating from the best publicized clowns of our society and from their fawns in the Fourth Estate.

Shakespeare, "King Lear," Act 2, Scene 2:

OSWALD: What dost thou know me for?

KENT: A knave, a rascal, an eater of broken meats; a base, proud, shallow, beggarly, three-suited, hundred-pound, filthy worsted-stocking knave; a lily-liver'd, action-taking, whoreson, glass-gazing, superserviceable, finical rogue; one-trunk inheriting slave; one that wouldst be a bawd in way of good service, and art nothing but the composition of a knave, beggar, coward, pander, and the son and heir of a mongrel bitch; one whom I will beat into clamorous whining if thou deniest the least syllable of thy addition.

mycterismos

mic-ter-is'mos

A common figure for the graffiti adorning public lava-
tories. Literally, the act of micturition (showering the
dew of one's kidneys) upon one's opponent. The figure
may be explicit or merely suggested.

Clemenceau:

Si je pouvais pisser comme Lloyd George parle.

Ralph Nader:

It is a crime for a man to relieve himself in the Detroit
River, but not for an industry to relieve itself in the
Detroit River. It costs twenty-five dollars to drop a banana
peel in Yosemite. But what fines have been levied for all
the havoc [offshore oil-drilling leaks] in Santa Barbara?

*Senator Carter Glass of Virginia, rebutting an attack on
Woodrow Wilson by Senator Gerald Nye (1936):*

. . . what I feel like saying here or elsewhere to the
man who thus insults the memory of Woodrow Wilson
is something which may not be spoken here, or printed in
the newspapers, or uttered by a gentleman.

Hosea Williams:

I am black and I am proud. I am black and I know that I am beautiful. Me being black and beautiful does not make white folks ugly just because they are white. Now there are some ugly white folks. I think that Lester Maddox [ex-governor of Georgia] is a very ugly man. I think that U.S. Attorney General Mitchell is a very ugly man. And, in fact, Richard Nixon is ugly, too.

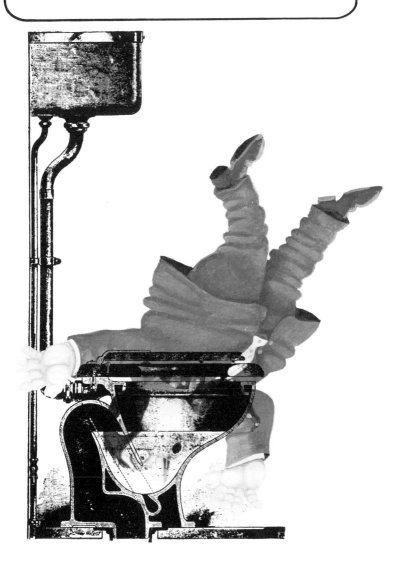

hyperbole

hī-per′bō-lē

A lie without intent to deceive. An expression of truth without facts to support it — the greater the innocent deception, the greater the truth.

Francis Bacon:

The speaking in perpetual hyperbole is comely in nothing but love.

Fred Allen:

He is so narrow-minded that if he fell on a pin, it would blind him in both eyes.

Eric Hoffer:

The young are slovenly and stoned, decked out in nightmarish masquerade on its way to the ashcan.

Malcolm X:

Give it to us yesterday, and that's not fast enough.

apophasis

a-pof'a-sis

The speaker begins his attack upon his adversary by saying that he is at a loss for words. The figure stirs up two implications: (a) that the faults of the adversary are so well known, they hardly need to be recited; (b) there are so many faults that any recitation of them will be incomplete.

Clarence Darrow, beginning his summation to the mine commission in a hearing that pitted owners against miners during the Pennsylvania coal strikes of 1903:

I scarcely know what to say in opening this case. (Thereupon, Darrow inveighed against the mine owners for the next eight hours.)

aeschrologia

es"-krō-lō'ji-a

A figure of derogation whose explicit terms offend public taste or the listener's ear.

Allegations from a lawsuit instigated by an ad hoc citizens' group in 1940 to bar philosopher Bertrand Russell from accepting an appointment at the City College of New York:

Russell] . . . lecherous, salacious, libidinous, lustful, venerous, erotomaniac, aphrodisiac, atheistic, irreverent, narrow-minded, untruthful and bereft of moral fibre. . . .

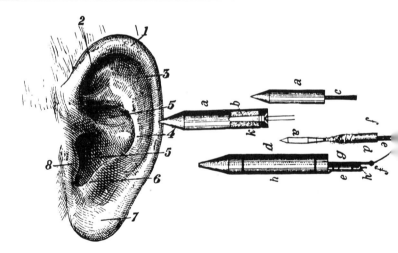

William Allen White, concerning H. L. Mencken:

With a pig's eyes that never look up, with a pig's snout that loves muck, with a pig's brain that knows only the sty, and a pig's squeal that cries only when he is hurt, he sometimes opens his big mouth, tusked and ugly, and lets out the voice of God, railing at the whitewash that covers the manure about his habitat.

dialysis

dī-al′i-sis

Two sides of a much-discussed issue are proposed by the speaker and rejected.

Eric Severeid on dissent in America:

. . . I do not subscribe to the proposition that if dissent is good in principle, then therefore the more dissent the better. I do not accept the argument of many youthful protesters that because the *right* of dissent is sacred, therefore the might and form of their dissent are sacred.

epicrisis

e-pi-crī'sis

To praise or derogate by means of a quote or paraphrase of another's thought.

Socialist Labor Party Platform, 1968:

"There is in the land a certain restlessness, a questioning." The words were uttered by President Johnson in his January 17, 1968, State of the Union Message. They understate the case. The American people are assailed by foreboding and bitterness, frustration and fear, bewilderment and doubt.

Fred Foy, Chairman, Koppers Company, to a meeting of businessmen:

You are a bunch of bums. Your character and morals are questionable. Your achievements have contributed mostly to discontent and confusion. You have been weighed and found wanting. The report is in, and it says that you are a pack of money-grabbing hyenas — your hearts pump to the rhythm of the cash register. You are interested only in your petty schemes. You have no use for your neighbors, except as consumers in an overstimulated economic system. . . . You are outmoded and old-fashioned, guilty of such stupidities as ambition, competitiveness and patriotism. . . . I hope I don't have to tell you that this is not my assessment. It comes from an important sub group in our society: the dissident young . . . and they have risen up in their uninformed wisdom and pronounced us a collective loss.

ethopoeia
e"-thō-pō'ya

An assessment of the adversary is formed through vivid, derisive detail concerning his mannerisms, proclivities, actions.

Josh Billings about Yankees:

The oil ov ther langwidge iz ther dezire tew pleze, and ther greezy words foreshadder a proffit.

Dylan Thomas on the riders of the lecture circuit:

There they go, every Spring, from New York to Los Angeles: exhibitionists, polemicists, histrionic publicists, theological rhetoricians, historical hoddy-doddies, balletomanes, ulterior decorators, windbags and bigwigs and humbugs, men in love with stamps, men in love with steaks, men after millionaires' widows, men with elephantiasis of the reputation (huge trunks and teeny minds), authorities on gas, bishops, best-sellers, editors looking for writers, writers looking for publishers, publishers looking for dollars, existentialists, serious physicists with nuclear missions, men from the B.B.C. who speak as though they had the Elgin marbles in their mouths, pot-boiling philosophers, professional Irishmen (very lepri-corny), and I am afraid, fat poets with slim volumes.

deisis

dē-ī'sis

An earnest request, often expressed as a prayer.

Senator Albert Beveridge, imploring the Senate to retain the Philippines:

The Philippines are ours forever, "territory belonging to the U.S.," as the Constitution calls them. And just beyond the Philippines are China's illimitable markets. We will not retreat from either. We will not repudiate our duty in the archipelago. We will not abandon our opportunity in the Orient. We will not renounce our part in the mission of our race, trustee, under God, of the civilization of the world. And we will move forward to our work, not howling out regrets like slaves whipped to their burdens, but with gratitude for a task worthy of our strength, and thanksgiving to Almighty God that He has marked us as His chosen people, henceforth to lead in the regeneration of the world.

eucharistia

ū-ka-ris'ti-a

A figure of praise whereby the speaker, in allowing for the confusion of his emotions and his inability to reciprocate what has been given, makes the givers appear infinitely generous. A popular figure for thank-you notes and testimonial banquets.

William Shakespeare:

Beggar that I am, I am even poor in thanks.

Sir Roger Casement, upon receiving the sentence of death for treason as a result of his participation in the Irish Easter Rising of 1916:

Gentlemen of the jury, I wish to thank you for your verdict. I hope you will not take amiss what I said, or think that I made any imputation upon your truthfulness or your integrity when I spoke and said that this was not a trial by my peers. I maintain that I have a natural right to be tried in that natural jurisdiction, Ireland, my own country, and I would put it to you, how would you feel in the converse case, or rather how would all men here feel in the converse case, if an Englishman had landed here in England and the Crown or the Government, for its own purposes, had conveyed him secretly from England to Ireland under a false name, committed him to prison under a false name, and brought him before a tribunal in Ireland under a statute which they knew involved a trial before an Irish jury? How would you feel as Englishmen if that man was to be submitted to trial by jury in a land inflamed against him and believing him to be a criminal, when his only crime was that he cared for England more than for Ireland?

hypotyposis

hī" pō-ti-pō'sis

A vivid depiction of what has been, is, or may be —
together with their causes and consequences. Almost
always implied in this figure is the proposition: "If
. . . then. . . ."

"The Ecologist," *a London magazine, January 1972:*

If current trends are allowed to persist, the breakdown of
society and the irreversible disruption of the life-support
systems on this planet — possibly by the end of the
century, certainly within the lifetime of our children —
are inevitable.

Judge Learned Hand:

. . . we rose from the ape because, like him, we kept
"monkeying around," always meddling with everything
about us. True, there is a difference, because, although
the ape meddles, he forgets, and we have learned, first to
meddle and remember, and then to meddle and record.
But without the meddling nothing would have happened
of all that glorious array of achievement: battleships,
aeroplanes, relativity, the proton, neutron and electron,
T.N.T., poison gas, sulfathiazole, the Fifth Symphony,
The Iliad, The Divine Comedy, Hamlet, Faust, The
Critique of Pure Reason, Das Kapital, the Constitution
of the United States, the Congress of Industrial Organiza-
tions, Huey Long, and the New Deal. All these from just
"monkeying around!"

Whitney M. Young:

There comes a time in the life of every great nation when it finds itself at the crossroads — on one side, the path of division, decline, oblivion; on the other, the path of progress, purpose and decency. There is every indication that this nation, almost two centuries after its birth by fire, is at the crossroads. At every hand we see the chaos instead of concern, drift instead of decision, and hate instead of hope. It may well be that we are witnessing the exhaustion of the American spirit; the full-scale retreat by a people nurturing false dreams of superiority; a retreat from the responsibilities and decency that characterize true greatness.

Thomas Jefferson, during the American Revolution:

The spirit of the times may alter, will alter. Our rulers will become corrupt, our people careless. A single zealot may become persecutor, and better men his victims. It can never be too often repeated that the time for fixing essential right, on a legal basis, is while our rulers are honest, ourselves united. From the conclusion of this war we shall be going downhill. It will not then be necessary to resort every moment to the people for support. They will be forgotten, therefore, and their rights disregarded. They will forget themselves in the sole faculty of making money and will never think of uniting to effect a due respect for their rights. The shackles, therefore, which shall not be knocked off at the conclusion of this war, will be heavier and heavier, till our rights revive or expire in a convulsion.

meiosis

mī-ō′sis

A cutting, double-edged figure. One side slices by means of exaggerated understatement; the other diminishes an opponent by means of an incorrect word or phrase, especially if it highlights a fault of the opponent. Thus, a speaker may strike at an adversary known for his height as "a little man," deride an enraged militant as "a nervous Nelly."

William Shakespeare, 94th sonnet:

F or sweetest things turn sour by their deeds,
Lilies that fester smell far worse than weeds.

Oscar Wilde:

One should not be too severe on English novels; they are only the relaxation of the intellectually unemployed.

Edgar Johnson, American-born authority on 19th-century English literature:

Dickens and Thackeray and Sydney Smith and Leigh Hunt and Walter Savage Landor are just as interesting to be spending your time with as Attorney General Mitchell.

encomion

en·kō'·mi·on

A generous heaping up of praise, usually on someone
of uncommon virtue.

William Wordsworth, "To Toussaint L'Ouverture":

Toussaint, the most unhappy man of men!
  Whether the whistling Rustic tend his plow
Within thy hearing, or thy head be now
Pillowed in some deep dungeon's earless den;
O miserable Chieftain! where and when
Wilt thou find patience! Yet die not; do thou
Wear rather in thy bonds a cheerful brow:
Though fallen thyself never to rise again,
Live, and take comfort. Thou hast left behind
Powers that will work for thee: air, earth, and skies;
There's not a breathing of the common wind
That will forget thee; thou hast great allies;
Thy friends are exultations, agonies,
And love, and man's unconquerable mind.

prosopopeia

pr̄o-s̄o-p̄o-p̄e′ya

A figure gauged to attain the heights of sublimity. Vigor is achieved by investing the inanimate with human qualities or by boldness of thought.

Robert Ingersoll:

I suppose it can truthfully be said that Hope is the only universal liar who never loses his reputation for veracity.

Charlie Chaplin, from his movie, **The Great Dictator:**

The misery that has come upon us is but the passing of greed — the bitterness of men who fear the way of human progress. The hate of men will pass.

You, the people, have the power — the power to create machines. The power to create happiness! You, the people, have the power to make this life free and beautiful — to make this life a wonderful adventure. Then — in the name of democracy — let us use that power — let us all unite.

Let us fight for a new world — a decent world that will give men a chance to work — that will give youth a future and old age a security.

Now let us fight to free the world — to do away with national barriers — to do away with greed, with hate and intolerance. Let us fight for a world of reason — a world where science and progress will lead to the happiness of us all.

categoria

ka-tē-gō'ri-a

Direct exposure of an adversary's faults.

President John F. Kennedy:

My father always told me that all businessmen were sons-of-bitches, but I never believed it till now.

Richard Rush on John Randolph, the first advocate of "strict constructionism"; the two were fellow Princeton graduates and members of the U.S. House of Representatives around 1830:

Never was ability so much below mediocrity so well rewarded; no, not even when Caligula's horse was made a consul.

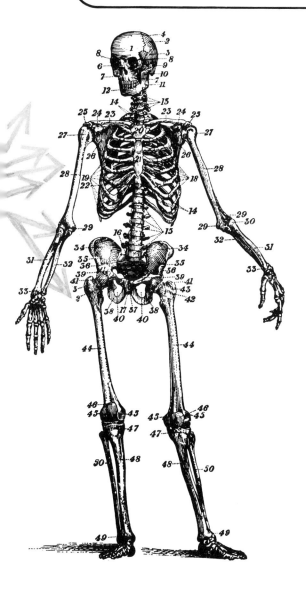

eustathia

yu-stā-thi-ä

To suggest or assert the unmovability of one's position, even in the face of the threat of torture or death.

Governor Winthrop Rockefeller, announcing his opposition to the death penalty:

What earthly mortal has the omnipotence to say who among us shall live and who shall die? I do not. Moreover, I cannot and will not turn my back on lifelong Christian teachings and beliefs, merely to let history run out its course on a fallible and failing theory of punitive justice.

Senator Russell Long, in response to plans by President Kennedy to cut off funds to school districts practicing segregation:

I expect to fight this proposition until hell freezes over. Then I propose to start fighting on the ice.

Declaration of Independence:

And, for the support of this declaration, with a firm reliance on the protection of Divine Providence, we mutually pledge to each other our lives, our fortunes, and our sacred honor.

analogia

an-a-lō'jä

Praiseworthiness or vice established by association. Because two qualities are alike, those who possess these qualities are, by extension, alike.

Gore Vidal:

Actors are like politicians and politicians are like actors. They both spend time each day contemplating their image. They both have a desire to be loved.

John Selden, ca. 1654:

In troubled water you can scarce see your face, or see it very little, till the water be quiet and stand still. So in troubled times you can see little truth; when times are quiet and settled, then truth appears.

oxymoron
ok-si-mō'ron

A figure designed to convey a truth by linking terms or phrases that are contradictory.

Ralph Waldo Emerson:

Extremes meet, and there is no better example than the haughtiness of humility.

Thomas Hobbes:

Force, and fraud, are in war the two cardinal virtues.

Congressman Edward I. Koch:

The fact that we will give a tax break to the inventor of a hair curler but not a composer of a musical score speaks poorly for the values of our society.

Louis Ginsberg:

Only in fetters is liberty:
Without its banks could a river be?

Spiro Agnew:

Protest is every citizen's right; but that does not insure that every protest is right.

Thomas De Quincy:

Here, reader, are some extraordinary truths, looking so very like falsehoods that you would never take them for anything else if you were not invited to give them special examination.

Justice Oliver Wendell Holmes:

It is only by effort that a man achieves the inevitable.

also . . . deafening silence, 'O miserable abundance,' the living dead, make haste slowly, sweet pain . . .

threnos

thrā'nos

Misery seeks company! The speaker is the center of this figure for commiseration.

President Warren Harding:

My god, this is a hell of a job! I have no trouble with my enemies. I can take care of them all right. But my damn friends, my god-damn friends . . . they're the ones that keep me walking the floor nights.

President Harry Truman:

To be President of the United States is to be lonely, very lonely at times of great decisions.

ecphonesis

ek-fo-nē'sis

A figure expressing deep feeling designed to arouse the same or yet more profound emotion.

Daniel O'Connell, during the 1924 battles against the British for Catholic emancipation in Ireland:

The Irish were made more thirsty for liberty by the drop that fell on their parched lips.

William Faulkner, on accepting the Nobel Prize in 1950:

I decline to accept the end of man. It is easy enough to say that man is immortal simply because he will endure: that when the last ding-dong of doom has clanged and faded from the last worthless rock hanging tideless in the last red and dying evening, that even then there will be one more sound: that of his puny inexhaustible voice, still talking. I refuse to accept this. I believe that man will not merely endure: he will prevail.

asphalia

as-fāl-ya

Equivalent to a money-back guarantee if not satisfied.
Assertions are warranted personally by the speaker.

William Makepeace Thackeray, concerning the English:

I say to you that you are better than a Frenchman. I would lay even money that you who are reading this are more than five feet even in height, and weigh eleven stone; while a Frenchman is five feet four and does not weigh nine. The Frenchman has after his soup a dish of vegetables, where you have one of meat. You are a different and superior animal. . . .

Sophie Tucker:

Honey, I've been rich.
Honey, I've been poor.
Believe me, honey,
Rich is best.

George Washington, on accepting appointment as Commander-in-Chief, June 1775:

. . . I beg leave to assure the Congress that as no pecuniary consideration could have tempted me to accept this arduous employment at the expense of my domestic ease and happiness, I do not wish to make any profit from it.

dodge
&
face up

pareuresis

pa-rū-rā'sis

The speaker offers an explanation for his views, course, or action, making up so compelling a justification that possible complaints and objections are nipped in the bud.

Rhode Island Congressman J. E. Fogarty, sponsor of the "Older Americans Act of 1965," on the day the law was enacted:

I don't like the phrase "older Americans." I don't like the phrase "senior citizens." But we had to give a name to a group of people that are being squeezed out of American life like a tube of toothpaste that's come to the end.

John Gardner:

The society which scorns excellence in plumbing because plumbing is a humble activity and tolerates shoddiness in philosophy because it is an exalted activity will have neither good plumbing nor good philosophy. Neither its pipes nor its theories will hold water.

Woodrow Wilson:

A man's rootage is more important than his leafage.

hypophora

hī-pof'ō-rä

By anticipating objections and answering them, the speaker obliges the listener to face up to and look more favorably on the position being advocated.

Tennessee Williams:

Whether or not we admit it to ourselves, we are all haunted by a truly awful sense of impermanence. I have always had a particularly keen sense of this at New York cocktail parties, and perhaps this is why I drink the martinis almost as fast as I can snatch them from the tray.

Shakespeare, **Julius Caesar,** *Act 3, Scene 2:*

If there be any in this assembly, any dear friend of Caesar's, to him I say that Brutus' love to Caesar was no less than his. If then that friend demand why Brutus rose against Caesar, this is my answer — not that I loved Caesar less, but that I loved Rome more.

Charles A. Lindbergh, when in the face of popular opposition he urged isolationism, 1941:

I know I will be severely criticized by the interventionists in America when I say we should not enter a war unless we have a reasonable chance of winning. That, they will claim, is far too materialistic a viewpoint. . . . And I know that the United States is not prepared to wage a war in Europe successfully at this time. We are no better prepared than France was when the interventionists in Europe persuaded her to attack the Siegfried Line.

dichaeologia

di·kī·a·lō′jä

In defense of one's blemished reputation or failings, to place the blame on extenuating circumstances, bad information furnished by sly enemies, betrayal by subordinates or former friends.

Richard M. Nixon, on the "hostile" American press:

You won't have Nixon to kick around any more.

Sam Rayburn:

Any jackass can kick down a barn, but it takes a good carpenter to build one.

Senator Barry M. Goldwater:

I won't say that the papers misquote me, but I sometimes wonder where Christianity would be today if some of those reporters had been Matthew, Mark, Luke or John.

President Franklin D. Roosevelt:

The Republican leaders have not been content to make personal attacks on me — or my wife — or my sons — they now include my little dog, Fala. Unlike the members of my family, Fala resents this. When he learned that the Republican fiction writers had concocted a story that I had left him behind on an Aleutian island and had sent a destroyer back to find him — at a cost to the taxpayer of two or three or twenty million dollars — his Scotch soul was furious. He has not been the same dog since. I am accustomed to hearing malicious falsehoods about myself, but I think I have a right to object to libelous statements about my dog.

diasyrmos

dī-a-sir'mos

Highlighting an assertion by comparing it with something base or ridiculous.

George Santayana:

To call war the soil of courage and virtue is like calling debauchery the soil of love.

Susan B. Anthony, on women's rights, 1873:

The only question left to be settled now is: Are women persons? And I hardly believe any of our opponents will have the hardihood to say that they are not.

from **"Black Politics: a Journal of Liberation,"** *1968:*

WE FAVOR GUN CONTROL LAWS THAT WILL PROVIDE EVERY BLACK ADULT, FREE OF CHARGE, A RIFLE AND HANDGUN FROM THE FEDERAL GOVERNMENT UNTIL THE DANGER OF ATTACK BY RACISTS OF ANY KIND IS OVER.

paramologia

pa-ra-mō-lō'jä

To confess one's faults, and in so doing, divert the issue or reflect adversely on an opponent.

President George Washington:

That I have foibles, and perhaps many of them, I shall not deny. I should esteem myself, as the world also would, vain and empty, were I to arrogate perfection. Knowledge in military matters is to be acquired by practice and experience only; and, if I have erred, great allowance should be made for the want of them; unless my errors should appear to be willful?

President Andrew Johnson:

I do not forget that I am a mechanic. I am proud to own it. Neither do I forget that Adam was a Tailor, sewing fig leaves together for aprons; Tubal Cain was an artificer in brass and iron; Joseph the husband of Mary was a carpenter, and our Saviour probably followed the same trade; the apostle Paul was a tentmaker; Socrates was a sculptor; Archimedes was a mechanic; King Crispin was a shoemaker; and so was Roger Sherman, who helped to form the Constitution.

John V. Lindsay, campaign theme during New York City's Mayoralty election of 1969:

I have made mistakes, but . . .

aposiopesis
ap″ō-sī-ō-pē′sis

An abrupt switch to another subject, caused by an adversary's word or deed that so troubles or angers the speaker as to require abandonment of his previous point. The figure generates suspicion toward the adversary and places blame on him for the speaker's choked-up feelings.

Attorney William M. Kunstler, in defense of the Chicago 8 on charges of conspiracy, 1970:

I am trembling because I am so outraged. I haven't been able to get this out before, and I am saying it now, and then I want you to put me in jail if you want to.

Joseph N. Welch to Senator Joseph McCarthy, during the 1954 hearings on charges of subversion in the Army:

Until this moment, Senator, I think I never really gauged your cruelty or your recklessness. . . . If it were in my power to forgive you for your reckless cruelty, I would do so. I like to think I'm a gentle man, but your forgiveness will have to come from someone other than me.

rift
&
meld

aenos
ē-nōs'

A figure designed to rally support among the erudite; a narration whose content is likely to be known only to the wise.

Father Daniel Berrigan:

It is a great and good thing, *dignum et justum*, when one's life is so impregnated with the values of a tradition, his life so colored, so impelled, so led as to be able to wrestle with the demons of his own (and others') lifetime. We shall see who emerges from the labyrinth: the minotaur or the man.

Poet John Ciardi:

One needs to hear Job lift his question into the wind; it is, after all, every man's question at some time. One needs to stand by Oedipus and hold the knife of his own most terrible resolution. One needs to come out of his own Hell with Dante and to hear that voice of joy hailing the sight of his own stars returned to. One needs to run with Falstaff, roaring in his own appetites and weeping into his own pathos. What one learns from these voices is his own humanity.

aporia

a-pō-ri-ä

A figure that begins with an assertion that the speaker is unfamiliar with the appropriate form for expressing his thought or feeling.

Letter to President Richard M. Nixon from Captain Aubrey M. Daniels III, prosecutor of Lt. William L. Calley, Jr., charged with involvement at the My Lai atrocities in Viet Nam:

Sir: It is very difficult for me to know where to begin this letter as I am not accustomed to writing letters of protest. I only hope that I can find the words to convey to you my feelings as a United States citizen, and as an attorney, who believes that respect for law is one of the fundamental bases upon which this nation is founded.

For this nation to condone the acts of Lieutenant Calley is to make us no better than our enemies and make any pleas by this nation for the humane treatment of our own prisoners meaningless.

I truly regret having to have written this letter and wish that no innocent person had died at My Lai on March 16, 1968. But innocent people were killed under circumstances that will always remain abhorrent to my conscience.

While in some respects what took place at My Lai has to be considered a tragic day in the history of our nation, how much more tragic would it have been for this country to have taken no action against those who were responsible.

That action was taken, but the greatest tragedy of all will be if political expediency dictates the compromise of such a fundamental moral principle as the inherent unlawfulness of the murder of innocent persons, making the action and the courage of six honorable men, who served their country so well, meaningless.

erotema

er-ō-tē'mä

To ask an unanswerable question. In this interrogative form of assertion, pity or anger may be aroused, an adversary embarrassed, reasonable people brought together on the side of the speaker.

Hugh Hefner:

There is something sick about a society that accepts detailed descriptions and images of human beings killing and maiming one another, but suppresses any too-precise picture or phrase about the physical act of love. What sort of society is it that tolerates violence, pain and the destruction of life in its books, magazines and movies, but is bothered by any too-intimate interest in an act of tenderness, pleasure and procreation?!

Martin Luther King, Jr., in an open letter to his "fellow clergymen":

In your statement you asserted that our actions, even though peaceful, must be condemned because they precipitate violence. Isn't this like condemning the robbed man because his possession of money precipitated the evil act of robbery? Isn't this like condemning Socrates because his unswerving commitment to truth and his philosophical delvings precipitated the misguided popular mind to make him drink the hemlock? Isn't this like condemning Jesus because his unique God-consciousness and never-ceasing devotion to God's will precipitated the evil act of the Crucifixion?

Senator Edward M. Kennedy:

How can the poor feel that they have a stake in a system which says that the rich may have due process but the poor may not? How can the uneducated have faith in a system which says that it will take advantage of them in every possible way?

taunt
&
balm

epiplexis

ep-i-plek'sis

Pinning down the opponent on specifics.

Statement by the American Civil Liberties Union:

Civilian and military intelligence agencies are spying on tens of thousands of law-abiding citizens — collecting, swapping and storing detailed data on their political and private lives. By the very act of snooping, these agencies caution the people. They warn they may sometime employ their force against individuals who lawfully use their freedoms of speech, conscience, press and assembly. The threat creates fear. Fear chills political dissent. And the chilling of dissent cracks the foundation of a democratic society, expanding the power of government beyond its lawful bounds to control its master, the people.

apologia

a-pōl-ō'-jä

A barbed truth is wrung from a fictional narration dealing with animals or unthinking things like parts of the body.

The vicar of St. Barnabas Church, Bolton, England:

The Bolton birds have begun courting. Will teenagers note that birds, except cuckoos, build their nests before hatching their eggs.

President John Adams:

The jaws of power are always open to devour, and her arm is always stretched out, if possible to destroy the freedom of thinking, speaking, and writing.

antanaclasis

ant-an-ak'la-sis

A figure in which a word is used more than once but with different meanings; a play on words that is ill-suited for serious comment. It is a twit delivered with a light touch.

Oliver Wendell Holmes:

Man wants little drink below, but wants that little strong.

Benjamin Franklin:

He that takes a wife takes care.

If we don't hang together, we'll hang separately.

Ambrose Bierce:

Here's to women! Would that we could fall into her arms without falling into her hands.

John Kendrick Bangs:

Pandemonium did not reign; it poured.

sarcasmos

sär-kaz'mos

A bitter taunt disguised in the garb of gentle wit; the object — to deride an opponent through laughter.

Winston Churchill, on Clement Attlee:

He was a modest man with much to be modest about.

Ambrose Bierce:

My advice to the women's clubs of America is to raise more hell and fewer dahlias.

Mark Twain:

There are 869 different forms of lying, but only one of them has been squarely forbidden. Thou shalt not bear false witness against thy neighbor.

Historian Charles Beard, on the McCarthy witch hunts of the 1950's:

You need only reflect that one of the best ways to get yourself a reputation as a dangerous citizen these days is to go about repeating the very phrases which our founding fathers used in the great struggle for independence.

asteismus

as-tēs′mus

An urbane pleasantry directed against an adversary, or which, when turned on oneself, tends to make the opponent appear ludicrous.

Elbert Hubbard:

A conservative is a man who is too cowardly to fight and too fat to run.

antiphrasis

an-tif'ra-sis

To taunt an opponent by means of a word or phrase that is an obvious contradiction of what is meant. Hence, the village fool is called the town sage, the town bully — a man of peace.

Malcolm X:

. . . brothers and sisters, friends and enemies, I just can't believe everyone in here is a friend and I don't want to leave anyone out.

Thomas Babington Macaulay, in a one-line review of Atterbury's **A Defense of the Licens of Phalaris:**

It really deserves the praise, whatever the praise may be worth, of being the best book ever written by any man on the wrong side of the question of which he was profoundly ignorant.

ironia

ī-rŏ'ni-ä

By tone of voice or gesture, the speaker obliges the listener to understand the opposite of what is said.

George Bernard Shaw:

Martyrdom is the only way in which a man can become famous without ability.

Thomas Wolfe, **Look Homeward, Angel:**

By Spring, if God was good, all the proud privileges of trench lice, mustard gas, splattered brains, punctured lungs, ripped guts, asphyxiation, mud, and gangrene, might be his.

Holbrook Jackson:

The poor are the only consistent altruists. They sell all that they have and give to the rich.

tattle
&
demurral

memphis
mem'fis

An impassioned summons for help for an expressed or implied complaint.

Lyman Beecher, American theologian and preacher, ca. 1850:

Oh Lord, grant that we may not despise our rulers: and grant, oh Lord, that they may not act so we can't help it.

Oliver Cromwell:

I beseech you, in the bowels of Christ, think it possible you may be mistaken?

paradoxon

pa·ra·dok′·son

A hesitation to affirm something as true, since the speaker would not have believed it to be so.

Bertrand Russell:

Although this may seem a paradox, all exact science is dominated by the idea of approximation.

Benjamin Disraeli:

"Frank and explicit" — this is the right line to take when you wish to conceal your own mind and to confuse the minds of others.

mimesis

mī-mē'sis

By means of mimicry or the gross imitation of mannerisms, habits of speech, appearance, or gesture, an opponent is derided.

Congressman F. Edward Hébert, 1971, on the introduction of mod fashion in the military:

I'm shaking in my boots. I'm scared to death. When you turn the military into a country club, discipline goes out the window. The military is not a democracy. Are we going to have mini-skirts in the mess halls? Will the commanding officer and the enlisted men pass each other and give a wave and say "Hi, toots?" They'll get so soft, they won't get dirt on their hands.

boost
&
bust

litotes

lit'-o-tēs

To exaggerate a fault or virtue by means of moderate understatement; or, with few words, to convey the impression of saying a great deal.

Reverend Charles Caleb Colton:

Many books require no thought from those who read them, and for a very simple reason — they made no such demand upon those who wrote them.

J. D. Salinger, Catcher in the Rye:

It isn't very serious. I have this tiny little tumor on the brain.

Henry Wadsworth Longfellow:

He speaketh not; and yet there lies a conversation in his eyes.

President Woodrow Wilson:

The best way to silence any friend of yours whom you know to be a fool is to induce him to hire a hall.

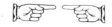

J. Robert Oppenheimer, on Einstein:

Any man whose errors take ten years to correct is quite a man.

protrope

pro-tro'pe

An exhortation to act, with the reasons for the appeal.

President Theodore Roosevelt:

Get action. Do things; be sane, don't fritter away your time; create, act, take a place wherever you are and be somebody; get action.

Prohibition Party Platform, 1968:

The liquor traffic is linked with and supports a nation-wide network of gambling, vice and crime. It also dominates both major political parties and, thru them, much of the governmental and political life of our nation. As long as the two dominant parties are largely controlled by the liquor traffic, just so long will they be unable to make moral principles prevail. The Prohibition Party alone offers a program to deal with this greatest of social ills. We urge all Americans who favor sobriety and righteousness to join with us in electing an Administration pledged to the above program.

President Franklin Delano Roosevelt, in his second inaugural speech, 1936:

It will take courage to let our minds be bold and find ways to meet the needs of the nation. . . . Here are thousands of men and women laboring for long hours in factories for inadequate pay — now!

. . . Here are thousands upon thousands of children who should be in school, working in mines and mills — now!

. . . Here are Spring floods threatening to roll again down our river valleys — now!

If we would keep faith with those who had faith in us, if we would make democracy succeed, I say we must act — now!

antenagoge

an-ten'a-gō-jä

The speaker concedes his past mistakes and, in so doing, reveals his good qualities or, by contrast, the faults of his adversaries.

John Brown, Harper's Ferry, 1859, upon receiving the death sentence:

I have, may it please the Court, a few words to say. In the first place, I deny everything but what I have all along admitted: of a desire on my part to free slaves.

John Nance Garner:

Worst damfool mistake I ever made was letting myself be elected Vice-President of the United States. Should have stuck with my old chores as Speaker of the House. I gave up the second most important job in the government for one that didn't amount to a hill of beans. I spent eight long years as Mr. Roosevelt's spare tire. I might still be Speaker if I hadn't let them elect me Vice-President.

Richard M. Nixon, 1952, in response to criticism regarding his political slush fund:

One thing I probably should tell you, because if I don't they'll probably be saying this about me too: We did get something — a gift — after the election. A man down in Texas heard Pat on the radio mention the fact that our two youngsters would like to have a dog. And, believe it or not, the day before we left on this campaign trip we got a message from Union Station in Baltimore saying they had a package for us. We went down to get it. You know what it was? It was a little cocker spaniel dog in a crate that had been sent all the way from Texas. Black and white spotted. And our little girl — Tricia, the six-year-old — named it Checkers. And you know the kids love the dog, and I just want to say this right now, that regardless of what they say about it, we're going to keep it.

John Haynes Holmes, America's leading liberal clergyman in 1939, after the signing of the Hitler-Stalin pact:

If we liberals were right on certain single aspects of the Russian Revolution, we were wrong, disgracefully wrong, on the question as a whole. We were wrong because, in our . . . vision of a new world springing from the womb of this Russian experiment, we permitted ourselves to condone the wrongs that we knew must be wrongs.

eulogia

yu-lō'ji-ä

Warm praise for someone's goodness, usually at funerals, expressed in a manner designed to instill the
listener with inspiration, dedication to high purpose,
and a sense of his own goodness.

*Gouverneur Morris, January 1, 1804, at the funeral of
Alexander Hamilton:*

Gentlemen of the bar — you have lost your brightest
ornament. Cherish and imitate his example. While,
like him, with justifiable and with laudable zeal, you
pursue the interests of your clients, remember, like him,
the eternal principle of justice.

*Edward Everett, August 1, 1826, in memory of Thomas
Jefferson and John Adams, both of whom had died a few
weeks earlier on July 4th:*

The faithful marble may preserve their image; the en-
graven brass may proclaim their worth; but the hum-
blest sod of Independent America, with nothing but the
dew-drops of the morning to gild it, is a prouder mauso-
leum than kings or conquerors can boast. The country is

their monument. Its independence is their epitaph. But not to the country is their praise limited. The whole earth is the monument of illustrious men. Wherever an agonizing people shall perish, in a generous convulsion, for want of a valiant arm and a fearless heart, they will cry, in the last accents of despair, O for a Washington, an Adams, a Jefferson! Wherever a regenerated nation, starting up in the night, shall burst the links of steel that enchain it, the praise of our venerated fathers shall be remembered in their triumphal song!

Ossie Davis, 1965, at the funeral of Malcolm X:

If you knew him you would know why we must honor him: Malcolm was our manhood! This was his meaning to his people. And, in honoring him, we honor the best in ourselves. . . . However much we may have differed with him — or with each other about him and his value as a man — let his going from us serve only to bring us together, now. Consigning these mortal remains to earth, the common mother of all, secure in the knowledge that what we place in the ground is no more now a man — but a seed — which, after the winter of our discontent, will come forth again to meet us. And we will know him then for what he was and is — a Prince — our own black shining Prince! — who didn't hesitate to die, because he loved us so.

paraenesis

pa·ren'e·sis

The speaker delivers a warning in a manner that has the quality of a proverbial saying.

George Jessel:

If you haven't struck oil in five minutes, stop boring.

Senator Barry Goldwater:

I would remind you that extremism in the defense of liberty is no vice. And let me remind you also that moderation in the pursuit of justice is no virtue.

Senator G. M. McDuffee of South Carolina, 1831:

He who dallies is a dastard; he who doubts is damned.

a
copia
of
rhetorical
ornamentation

a copia

The word "copia" is borrowed from Desiderius Erasmus
of Rotterdam, illustrious philosopher, scholar, humanist,
and rhetorician of the sixteenth century. The word appears in the title of his book: *De Utreque Verborem ac
Rerum Copia*, published in 1514. Erasmus borrowed the
word from the title of a passage in the tenth book of Quintilian's Institutio oratoria: *De copia verborum*. Erasmus'
book was an effort to update rhetoric, to kindle a broader
interest in it, and to teach a mastery of the subject. As
used by Erasmus, *copia* suggests *variety* and the methods
for achieving variety through the arrangement of words.

In his book, actually a textbook on rhetoric, the
term "copia" also suggested the *ability* to enrich language
and thought through an understanding of how figures of
speech may be constructed, how these may best serve the
speaker's intentions, and the occasions most suited for
specific intentions and figures.

In the first part of our book we have dwelt on
figures that are clearly and cosily at home with a variety
of intentions. But there are many figures that do not
easily lend themselves to assignment to little boxes or
categories of human motivation. And so our *copia* stresses
figures that are primarily ornamental, figures that enrich
thought, provide variety, permit language to soar from
the page when printed, to echo eternally when spoken, to
delight at all times. The analytical reader of our book will
have already noticed that many a figure makes use of one
or more other devices that are presented in the copia; this
is how matters should be, for it is possible not only to
cloak a mystery in an enigma, but also to take a simple
ornamental figure and breathe into it the stuff of immortal
praise or vilification.

orcos

or'cōs

To affirm or deny a position by the expression of strong conviction or oath.

Oliver Wendell Holmes:

I firmly believe that if the whole *materia medica* could be sunk to the bottom of the sea, it would be all the better for mankind and all the worse for the fishes.

syllepsis

si-lep'sis

One word is used two or more times, with slightly different meanings, to clarify two or more other words.

Senator Barry Goldwater:

A government that is big enough to give you all you want is big enough to take it all away.

pragmatographia

prag·ma·tō·graf′ya

A vivid, image-generating, *cinéma-verité* depiction of a person or event.

Winston Churchill:

I see advancing . . . in hideous onslaught the Nazi war machine, with its clanking, heel-clicking, dandified Prussian officers, its crafty expert agents fresh from the cowing and tying-down of a dozen countries. I see also the dull, drilled, docile, brutish masses of the hun soldiery plodding on like a swarm of crawling locusts. I see the German bombers and fighters in the sky, still smarting from many a British whipping, delighted to find what they believe is an easier and safer prey. Behind all this glare, behind all this storm, I see that small group of villainous men who plan, organize and launch this cataract of horrors upon mankind.

antonomasia

an·ton·ō·mās·yä

A deliberate misnaming of somebody or something so that the person or thing is identified with the misnomer. Figures vary from lofty appellations that are ennobled by tradition, as in forms of address: "Mr. President," "your Honor," "my ball and chain," to such derogations as "handkerchief-head," "honky," "flatfoot," "Pollyanna," "bleeding heart." There are also "Romeos," "Svengalis," "shadow governments," "Mata Haris," as well as appellations created by deriving a noun from a verb: "Killer," "Fighting Bob," "Swinger."

William Allen White:

We are all the children of John Q. Public, and our interests as members of the consuming public are after all our chief end and objective as citizens of our democracy.

Malcolm X:

Your and my mother and father, who didn't work an eight-hour shift, but worked from "can't see" in the morning until "can't see" at night, worked for nothing, making the white man rich, making Uncle Sam rich.

also . . .

The New World / The American Dream / Old Glory / The Melting Pot / Dixie / Dullsville, U.S.A.

anadiplosis

an"a-di-plō'sis

When hammering home a point, the figure helps the cause of emphasis by repeating as the first word or sound of the last part of the expression, the last word or sound used in the first part.

Herman Wouk, **The Caine Mutiny:**

Aboard my ship, excellent performance is standard. Standard performance is sub-standard. Sub-standard performance is not permitted to exist.

J. Howard Griffin, **Black Like Me:**

The laughter had to be gross or it would turn to sobs, and to sob would be to realize, and to realize would be to despair.

polyptoton

pol-ip-tō'ton

A figure designed to delight the ear by repeating words in slightly varying grammatical forms, a gerund for its noun, an adverb for its verb, the present repeated in its past tense.

President Franklin D. Roosevelt:

Let me assert my firm belief that the only thing we have to fear is fear itself.

Joseph Wood Krutch:

But in this desert country, they may see the land being rendered useless by overuse.

metonymia

me-ton'im-ya

The use of a suggestive word for what is meant, substitution of the symbol of something for the thing itself: "brass" for military leaders, "bottle" and "John Barleycorn" for certain types of beverage.

Edna Ferber:

. . . if it's ever told straight, you'll know it's the sunbonnet and not the sombrero that has settled the country.

George Meany, AFL-CIO president, 1966:

Capital has learned to sit down with labor.

Arthur Guiterman:

The stones that critics hurl with harsh intent a man may use to build his monument.

President Lyndon B. Johnson:

Government is an Irish boy from Boston who grew up to be president. Government is the son of a German immigrant from Pekin, Illinois, who became a leader of the American Senate. Government is a rancher from Montana, a banker from New York, an automobile maker from Detroit; government is the son of a tenant farmer from Texas who is speaking to you tonight.

isodunamia

ī-sō-du-nām'yä

A sense of brief, intense contrariness is created by adding, taking away, or doubling a negative.

John Dryden:

No government has ever been, or ever can be, wherein time-servers and blockheads will not be uppermost.

John Ruskin:

. . . an uneducated person may know, by memory, many languages, and talk them all, and yet truly know not a word of any — not a word even of his own.

President Richard M. Nixon, 1972:

If we were indifferent to the shortcomings of our society or complacent about our institutions or blind to the lingering inequities, then we would have lost our way. But the fact that we have those concerns is evidence that our ideals, deep down, are still very strong. Indeed, they remind us that what is really best about America is compassion. They remind us that in the final analysis America is great. Not because it is strong, not because it is rich, but because this is a good country.

Let us reject the narrow visions of those who would tell us that we are evil because we are not perfect; that we are corrupt because we are not yet perfect; that all the sweat and toil and sacrifice that have gone into the building of America were for naught because the building is not yet done.

apodixis

ap-ō-dik'sis

Rejection of an opponent's arguments as lies, absurdity, or slander.

Spiro Agnew, in response to Senator Edmund Muskie's charge that President Nixon had led the country into the biggest economic disaster since the Great Depression:

Either his memory needs jogging, or his rhetorical glands need a checkup.

synecdoche

si-nek′dō-kē

A figure requiring the listener to grasp the whole from citation of a part, to understand things which follow from hints about what has preceded, or the reverse: the particular from the general, or the past from hints about the future.

President Franklin D. Roosevelt:

The hand that held the dagger has struck it into the back of its neighbor.

Samuel A. Duffield:

Every prison is the exclamation point and every asylum is the question mark in the sentences of civilization.

President Dwight David Eisenhower:

When we consider these things, then the valley of the Thames draws closer to the farms of Kansas.

Winston Churchill, addressing Congress, 1941:

Lastly, if you will forgive me for saying it, to me the best tiding of all, the United States, united as never before, has drawn the sword for freedom, and cast away the scabbard.

enthymeme
en'thi-mēm

Either through words or ideas the figure brings contraries together. Out of the seeming clash of contraries a meaning, beyond the words themselves, is stirred up and supplied by the listener.

Astronaut Neil Armstrong, on the moon July 20, 1969:

That's one small step for a man, one giant step for mankind.

Pope's Iliad *xiv:*

> Persuasive speech, and more persuasive sighs,
> Silence that speaks, and eloquence of eyes.

Charles Dickens:

It was the best of times, it was the worst of times. . . .

J. Robert Oppenheimer:

Our knowledge separates as well as unites; our orders disintegrate as well as bind; our art brings us together and sets us apart.

Christopher Morley:

All cities are mad: but the madness is gallant. All cities are beautiful, but the beauty is grim.

gnome

nōm

Introduction into any part of a discourse of a "wise" saying, on any subject and for any purpose, whether cogent or irrelevant. The more striking the gnome, the greater is the effect in highlighting how or what the speaker has already said or is about to say.

George Santayana:

The young man who has not wept is a savage, and the old man who will not laugh is a fool.

Gnomes range from a philosophical "kibbitz" and wise-crack to proverb and aphorism. Gnomes are multitudinous and multifarious, and distinctions among them — arbitrary. According to sagacious Oscar Levant, "an epigram is a wisecrack that's played Carnegie Hall," and for poet W. H. Auden an epigram differs from an aphorism only by the difference in generality between them, the former specific and limited in scope, the latter broad, even universal.

mythos

mē'thos

A narration of events, true or imagined, against the background of a fabulous, mythical, or legendary country. This is a favorite of parents describing childhood joys and sorrows.

Advertising slogan:

Come to Marlboro country!

President James A. Garfield:

An Englishman who was wrecked on a strange shore and wandering along the coast . . . came to a gallows with a victim hanging on it, and fell down on his knees and thanked God that he at last beheld a sign of civilization.

epitrope

e·pit′rō·pē

Conceding an argument or an important point in an argument to the opponent, if, by so doing, the opponent is made to appear the butt of a jest, or if the concession actually hurts the opponent's position.

Sir Thomas Browne:

'Tis true, there is an edge in all firm belief, and with an easy metaphor we may say the sword of faith.

Lord Justice Mackinnon, 1938:

We have listened to an ingenious argument by Mr. Schiller. That argument persuaded me of one thing —namely, that this case was arguable—but it did not persuade me of anything further. As the charm of his rhetoric fades away, I believe that I shall revert to the belief that this case was really unarguable.

exergasia

ex-er-gā'jä

To repeat a point but with slight variations to convey the impression of saying something new.

Aldous Huxley:

A bore is a person who drills a hole in your spirit, who tunnels relentlessly through your patience, through all the crusts of voluntary deafness, inattention, rudeness, which you vainly interpose — through and through, until he pierces to the very quick of your brain.

apomnemonsysis

a-pom'nē-mon-sī-sis

The speaker illuminates his position by quoting or referring to the thought or point of view of a well-known person, living or dead.

Henry Adams:

The mania for handling all the sides of every question, looking into every window, and opening every door, was, as Bluebeard judiciously pointed out to his wives, fatal to their practical usefulness in society.

Senator Eugene J. McCarthy:

We must not do the wrong things for the right reasons, nor succumb to what T. S. Eliot called the ultimate temptation, described by Thomas à Becket as he faced martyrdom: "The last temptation is the greatest treason: to do the right deed for the wrong reason." We must not betray ourselves or our beliefs. Even though we write the case against ourselves in the invisible ink of self-justification and self-righteousness, blackened by the acid of history, it will stand out against us and we will stand condemned in our own land.

Howard Mumford Jones, "Farewell" to the Harvard University English Department, January 12, 1963:

The soul of a people, the past to which it looks back with pride and affection — these are not found in its IBM machinery or its tariff laws or its military might, but in its language, its literature, its religion, its art. "Give me," cried Andrew Fletcher of Saltoun, "the making of the songs of a nation, and I care not who makes its laws." This famous sentence, simple and profound, is known to everybody except politicians and practical men, who look upon human beings as bodies to be moved around, fed, cajoled, housed, and if necessary, shot at and buried.

catacosmesis

ca-ta-cŏs-mē'sis

Placing, for the sake of emphasis or amplification, the weightier, more important words or ideas first and other ideas or words set in order of diminishing importance; or the reverse: the most important element appearing last.

William Lloyd Garrison:

I am in earnest — I will not equivocate — I will not excuse — I will not retreat a single inch — and I will be heard.

Malcolm X:

As long as the white man sent you to Korea, you bled. He sent you to Germany, you bled. He sent you to the South Pacific to fight the Japanese, you bled. You bleed for white people, but when it comes to seeing your own church being bombed and little black girls murdered, you haven't got any blood. You bleed when the white man says bleed, you bite when the white man says bite; and you bark when the white man says bark.

(Very versatile rhetorician, Malcolm X; the passage also uses anaphora, epanastrophe, epanadiplosis, parimion, asyndeton and syllepsis.)

antimetabole

an"ti-me-tab'-ō-lē

To add emphasis to words and phrases by repeating
them in reverse grammatical order.

Francis Bacon:

If we begin with certainties, we shall end in doubts; but
if we begin with doubts, and are patient in them, we
shall end in certainties.

President John F. Kennedy:

Ask not what your country can do for you; ask what you
can do for your country.

epizeuxis

ep-i-zūk'sis

Repetition of the same word or sound without an intervening one; the figure adds vehemence to expression. Note the difference in effect in the French "*O la*" from "*O la, la*" and in the Yiddish "*Oi!*" from "*Oi, oi, oi!*"

John C. Calhoun:

The cry of Union! Union! the glorious Union! can no more prevent disunion, than the cry of Health! Health! glorious Health! on the part of the physician can save a patient lying dangerously ill.

anamnesis

an-am-nē'sis

A summoning up of things past so that by their re-membrance, the speaker's thoughts are more fully expressed. According to rhetor laureate Thomas De Quincey, vivacity of memory is ". . . the true *fundus* from which understanding draws."

Thomas De Quincey, ca. 1847:

And, as regards myself, touch but some particular key of laughter and echoing of music, sound but for a moment one bar of preparation, and immediately the pomps and glory of all that has composed for me the delirious vision of life re-awaken for torment; the orchestras of the earth open simultaneously to my inner ear; and in a moment I behold, forming themselves into solemn groups and processions, and passing over sad phantom stages all, that chiefly I have loved, or in whose behalf chiefly I have abhorred and cursed the grave — all that should *not* have died, yet died the soonest — the brilliant, the noble, the wise, the innocent, the brave, the beautiful.

pysma

piz'ma

The repetitious use of questions to drive home the speaker's point.

Jacques Barzun, The American University:

Why do we do *this?* — is it the trustees? Why can't we do *that?* Doesn't the administration understand? Why weren't we told?" — after all, *we* are the university.

Fulton J. Sheen:

History? The British never remember it; the Irish never forget it; the Russians never make it; and the Americans never learn from it.

Mayor John V. Lindsay:

How much have we been able to change? Have we moved any closer to the American Dream? The dream tells us that America is a land of economic opportunity. The reality is a foreclosure sign on the house down the block and a jobless line on every main street. The dream tells us that America believes in the Bill of Rights. The reality is that phones are tapped and offices are bugged and the government of the people is spying on the representatives of the people.

Clarence Darrow, debate on capital punishment, 1924:

Do you think man, in any sense, is a creature of the environment? Do you think you people could, day by day, wish and hope and pray for the slaughter of thousands of Germans because they were your enemies, and not become callous to suffering? Do you think that children of our schools and Sunday schools could be taught killing and be as kindly and tender after it as before? Do you think man does not feel every emotion that comes to him, no matter from what source it comes? Do you think this war did not brutalize the hearts of millions of people in this world? And are you going to cure it by brutalizing it still more by capital punishment?

zeugma

zūg'mä

A figure in which a single verb dictates to two or more clauses; a prozeugma, if the verb appears at the beginning, mezzozeugma, if it is in the middle, and hypozeugma, at or near the end.

hypozeugma
John Milton, Paradise Lost:

> . . . when the Scourge inexorably,
> and the torturing houre
> calls us to Penance.

mezzozeugma
Samuel Butler:

People in general are equally horrified at hearing the Christian religion doubted, and at seeing it practiced.

prozeugma
Peter Cooper:

Let the schools teach the nobility of labor and the beauty of human service: but the superstitions of ages past? — never!

prosographia
prō-sō-graf'ya

A simple, precise description; a news photograph in words.

Helen Keller:

We walked down the path to the well-house, attracted by the fragrance of the honeysuckle with which it was covered. Someone was drawing water and my teacher placed my hand under the spout. As the cool stream gushed over one hand she spelled into the other the word *water*, first slowly and then rapidly. I stood still, my whole attention fixed upon the motion of her fingers. Suddenly I felt a misty consciousness as of something forgotten — a thrill of returning thought; and somehow the mystery of language was revealed to me. I knew then that "w-a-t-e-r" meant the wonderful cool something that was flowing over my hand. That living word awakened my soul, gave it light, joy, set it free!

epexergasia

ē-pex-er-gā'ja

The expression of a single point through a variety of repetitions.

Winston Churchill:

If you have an important point to make, don't try to be subtle or clever. Use a pile driver. Hit the point once. Then come back and hit it again. Then hit it a third time — a tremendous whack.

Allen Ginsberg:

We have an international youth society of solitary children — stilyagi, provo, beat, mufado, nadaista, energumeno, mod and rocker — all aghast at the space-age horror world they are born to, and not habituated to — and now questioning the nature of the universe itself, as is proper in the space age. . . . What satisfaction is now possible for the young? Only the satisfaction of their desire — love, the body, and orgy; the satisfaction of a peaceful natural community where they can circulate and explore persons, cities, and the nature of the planet; the satisfaction of encouraged self-awareness; and the satiety and cessation of desire, anger, grasping and craving.

orismos

or-is'mos

A pithy declaration of your subject, most concise, most precise, even if the statement suffers want of logic.

Alexander Berkman, social activist and anarchist:

In a nutshell, the meaning of Communist Anarchism is this: the abolition of government, of coercive authority and all its agencies, and joint ownership — which means free and equal participation in the general work and welfare.

symploche

sim'plō-kē

The first word in a succession of phrases or sentences is repeated at the beginning or at the end of phrases or sentences.

Mark Twain:

Hain't we got all the fools in town on our side? And ain't that a big enough majority for any town?

Eugene V. Debs:

While there is a lower class I am in it; while there is a criminal class I am of it. While there is a soul in prison, I am not free.

Eric Hoffer:

It seems that we are most busy when we do not do the thing we ought to do; most greedy when we cannot have the one thing we really want; most hurried when we can never arrive; most self-righteous when irrevocably in the wrong. There is apparently a link between excess and unattainability.

Robert M. La Follette, Milwaukee, 1902, summing up arguments for primary elections for the choice of candidates for public office:

The right to cast the ballot is regarded as sacred. The right to make the ballot is equally sacred. No man shall be compelled to delegate his power to make his ballot. Boss Tweed said, "You may elect whichever candidates you please to office, if you will allow me to select the candidates." The boss can always afford to say, "You may vote any ticket you please so long as I make all the tickets." The character of the men nominated and the influences to which they owe their nomination determine the character of government.

barbarismos

bar-bar-is'mos

A faulty arrangement produced either through grammatical vice or incorrect words — the effect on the listener is usually one of perplexity. If the figure is used deliberately, it is often referred to as "double-talk." Also, mimicry of foreign pronunciation or that of the uneducated.

Dwight D. Eisenhower, 1952:

W e are not going to let our citizens, through no fault of their own, fall down into disaster they could not have foreseen and due to the exigencies of our particular form of economy, this modern economy where they have no power to keep themselves out of that.

Petroleum V. Nasby, August 6, 1862, "Why he should not be drafted":

I dont suppose that my political opinions, wich are aginst the prossekooshn uv this unconstooshnel war, wood hev any wate, with a draftin orfiser; but the above reesons why I cany go, will, I make no doubt, be suffishent.

eclipsis

ē-clip'sis

Deliberate omission of a word or a thought that the listener supplies through ordinary understanding.

Frank McKinney:

There's another advantage of being poor — a doctor will cure you faster.

Abraham Lincoln:

What kills a skunk is the publicity it gives itself.

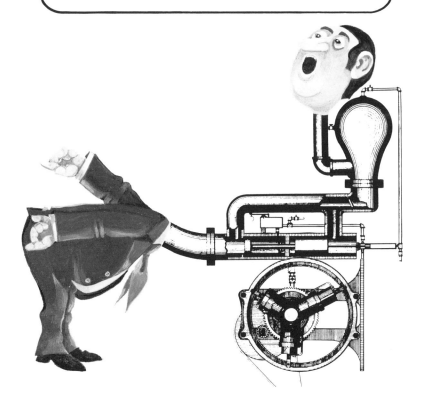

noema

nō-ēm'ä

A figure containing a deliberate bit of obscurity, whose meaning must be read between the lines, or grasped from the drift of it.

Robert S. McNamara, former Secretary of Defense:

To take no action is to take undecided action.

Wedding pledge of a young flower couple, 1971:

For better, for worse,
for richer, for poorer,
in sickness and in health,
against the war and in peace,
and as long
as we both shall dig it.

epiphonema

ep"i-fō-nē'ma

An exclamation or heightened feeling expressed in condensed form at the conclusion of an utterance.

John Ruskin:

And the great mistake of the best men through generation after generation, has been the great one of thinking to help the poor by almsgiving, and by preaching of patience or of hope and by every other means, emollient and consolatory, except the one thing which God orders for them, justice.

Justice Oliver Wendell Holmes, on his 90th birthday, March 7, 1931:

The riders of a race do not stop short when they reach the goal. There is a little finishing canter before coming to a standstill. There is time to hear the kind voices of friends and say to myself: The work is done. But just as one says that, the answer comes: The race is over, but the work never is done while the power to work remains. The canter that brings you to a standstill need not be only coming to rest. It cannot be, while you still live. For to live is to function. That is all there is to living. And so I end with a line from a Latin poet who uttered the message more than fifteen hundred years ago, "Death plucks my ear and says: Live — I am coming."

antitheton

an-ti-thē'ton

A figure wherein contrasting things with well-known qualities are allowed to collide elegantly.

W. M. Praed, 1825, on the death of the self-indulgent King George IV:

> A noble and nasty race he ran
> superbly filthy and fastidious;
> He was the world's first gentleman
> and made the appellation hideous.

Carl Van Doren:

The race of man, while sheep in credulity, are wolves for conformity.

Carl Sandburg, before a joint session of Congress on the 150th birthday of Abraham Lincoln:

Not often in the story of mankind does a man arrive on earth who is both steel and velvet, who is as hard as rock and soft as drifting fog, who holds in his heart and mind the paradox of terrible storm and peace unspeakable and perfect.

Paul Goodman:

Thus, my Apology for the literature to which I have devoted the years of my life is very like the others over several centuries, and it is noteworthy that they are all similar. Possibly if we had a very different kind of community, we would say something different; but possibly it is the human condition — how would I know? Literature confounds the personal and impersonal, meaning and beginning to act, and thought and feeling. In this confusion which is like actual experience, it makes a kind of sense. It imagines what might be, taking account of what is. Using the code of language, it continually revises the code to cope with something new. It is more conservative than science and more daring than science. It makes the assured and powerful uneasy, if only out of powerless spite. It speaks my common speech and it makes human speech noble. It provides a friendly community across ages and boundaries, and cheers my solitude. It is the way I pray to God and patriotically revere my background. It is legitimacy and rebellion.

euche

yu'ki

A promise, actual or implied, in a context in which the reasons for the promise are set forth.

John V. Lindsay, 1966:

I cannot promise you a peaceful, quiet administration. I cannot promise you that you will not continue to hear the howls of the power brokers. I cannot promise you the ominous silence of unanimity. But I can promise you change and reform and progress.

Adlai E. Stevenson:

I don't believe irresponsible promises are good politics. Promise-peddling and double talk may be expedient and catch some votes from the unwary and innocent, but promises also have a way of coming home to roost.

auxesis

ak-sē'sis

A figure that cumulates contraries.

Senator Ingalls, on "professional" political reformers of the 19th century:

. . . effeminate without being either masculine or feminine; unable either to beget or bear; possessing neither fecundity nor virility; endowed with the contempt of men and the derision of women, and doomed to sterility, isolation, and extinction.

dialogosismos

dī-a-lō-gō-sis'mus

Narration of an imagined conversation or correspondence with another person, and in the pretended dialogue, the speaker's views are set forth as well as those of the person imagined.

President Harry S Truman:

I heard a fellow tell a story about how he felt when he had to make speeches. He said when he has to make a speech, he felt like the fellow who was at the funeral of his wife, and the undertaker had asked him if he would ride down to the cemetery in the same car with his mother-in-law. He said, "Well, I can do it, but it's just going to spoil the whole day for me."

martyria

mar'tyr-ya

A figure of personal testimony, which gains credibility if the speaker is known to have lived through, rather than read through, a subject to become its master. It is a most persuasive figure, for it promotes the drawing of inferences from a speaker's unique experiences.

President John F. Kennedy:

Those of you who regard my profession of political life with some disdain should remember that it made it possible for me to move from being an obscure lieutenant in the United States Navy to Commander-in-Chief in fourteen years with very little technical competence.

Maurice Herzog, on his conquest of Annapurna, the Himalayan peak, 1950:

In my worst moments of anguish, I seemed to discover the deep significance of existence of which till then I had been unaware. I said that it was better to be true than to be strong. The marks of the ordeal are apparent on my body. I was saved and I had won my freedom. This freedom, which I shall never lose, has given me the assurance and serenity of a man who has fulfilled himself.

anaphora

an-af'ō'ra

By repeating the same word or phrase at the beginning of sentences, clauses, or paragraphs, the speaker obliges the listener to anticipate subsequent repetitions and the thoughts therein enmeshed.

Edmund Burke, on the impeachment of Warren Hastings:

It is a contradiction in terms, it is a blasphemy in religion, it is wickedness in politics, to say that any man can have arbitrary power.

President Warren G. Harding:

America's present need is not heroics but healing; not nostrums but normalcy; not revolutions but restoration; . . . not surgery but serenity.

Malcolm X:

Why should white people be running all the stores in our community? Why should white people be running the banks of our community? Why should the economy of our community be in the hands of the white man?

polysyndeton

pol·i·sin'de·ton

A high style of utterance for a low style of argument. A figure using numerous connecting links, sometimes the same, sometimes different, designed to produce vigor and emphasis.

Lord Eskgrove, condemning a tailor to death for murdering a soldier, 1856:

And not only did you murder him, whereby he was bereaved of his life, but you did thrust, or push, or pierce, or project, or propell the lethal weapon through the bellyband of the regimental breeches which were His Majesty's.

anastrophe

a-nas'trō-fē

To turn the usual order of words about, producing thereby some preposterous effect, which will elicit wonder, laughter, or simply a pause in the discourse.

V. S. Pritchett:

Rich, famous, proud, a ruling despot Pope might be — but he *was* middle class.

James Russell Lowell:

Talent is that which is in a man's power; genius is that in whose power man is.

asyndeton

a-sin'de-ton

Strength, vigor, and assurance are conveyed by omitting connecting parts of speech.

Democratic Party Platform, 1968:

We are an acting, doing, feeling people. We are a people whose deepest emotions, the source of the creative noise we make — precisely because of our ardent desire for unity, our wish for peace, our longing for concord, our demand for justice, our hope for material well-being, our impulse to move toward a more perfect union.

Spiro Agnew:

For too long — and this needs to be said and said now and here — the strength of freedom in our society has been eroded by a creeping permissiveness — in our legislatures, in our courts, in our family life, in our colleges and universities.

Eric Erikson:

From a genetic point of view, then, the process of identity formation emerges as an evolving configuration — a configuration which is gradually established by successive ego syntheses and re-syntheses throughout childhood; it is a configuration gradually integrating constitutional givens, idiosyncratic libidinal needs, favored capacities, significant identifications, effective defenses, successful sublimations, and consistent roles.

epanalepsis

ep"a-na-lep'sis

To place a word or phrase at the beginning of an expression and to repeat it at the end.

Benjamin Disraeli:

The services in war time are fit only for desperadoes, but in peace are fit only for fools.

President Thomas Jefferson:

Assuredly nobody will care for him who cares for nobody.

Benjamin Franklin:

They that give up essential liberty to obtain a little temporary safety deserve neither liberty nor safety.

epemboly

ē-pem'bō-lē

An insertion into the flow of discourse of material that may be alien to the subject. By means of such interruption, the speaker may make a pointed comment on some matter, amplify the discourse, or if the interruption is striking, add power to the main expression.

Samuel Johnson, "Life of Richard Savage":

But when Savage was provoked, and very small offenses were sufficient to provoke him, he would prosecute his revenge with the utmost acrimony till his passion had subsided.

onedismos

ō-ne·dis'mos

An opponent is derided for an act of ingratitude.

Senator George Henry Williams of Oregon, 1867:

The woman who undertakes to put her sex in the adversary position to man, who undertakes by the use of some independent political power to contend and fight against man, displays a spirit which would, if able, convert all the now harmonious elements of society into a state of war, and make every home a hell on earth.

parimion

pa-ri'mi-on

The several words of an expression begin with the same letter or sound; a way of promoting melody and sonority. Also known as alliteration.

William Allen White:

We have let the idea of freedom under self-respect go to seed in our colleges, and we are turning out too many hard-boiled, hard-hearted, hard-headed dumb-bells.

President Lyndon B. Johnson:

Today the cost of failure to communicate is not silence or serenity but destruction and disillusion.

Warren G. Harding, nominating William Howard Taft in 1912:

Progress is not proclamation or palaver. It is not pretense nor play on prejudice. It is not the perturbation of a people passion-wrought nor a promise proposed.

President John F. Kennedy:

Already American vessels had been searched, seized, and sunk.

metaplasmos

me-ta-plas'mos

A general principle for fashioning figures of speech. If the pristine word is found wanting, a letter or a syllable may be added, taken away, or juxtaposed in order to fulfill the speaker's intent more adequately.

RULES FOR METAPLASMOTIC MANEUVERS

PROTHESIS

add at the beginning

APHORESIS

remove from the beginning

EPENTHESIS

add in the middle

SYNCOPE

take from the middle

PARAGOGE

add at the end

APOCOPE

take from the end

SYSTOLE

shorten a long syllable

SYNALAEPHA

lengthen a short syllable

DIAERSIS

to make two syllables of one

ANTISTOECON

changing letters

METATHESIS

to transpose letters or syllables